To my lovely friend, Helena P., the most beautiful butterfly in the garden.
Thank you for always flying by my side. – *Rena Ortega*

To my lovely daughters, Sabina and Diana, who have
accompanied me on many expeditions to study butterflies.
I hope we keep exploring, discovering, and marvelling together. – *Roger Vila*

Translated from the Spanish *Mariposas, vida secreta* by Paula Meiss

First published in the United Kingdom in 2022 by
Thames & Hudson Ltd, 181A High Holborn, London WC1V 7QX

First published in the United States of America in 2022 by
Thames & Hudson Inc., 500 Fifth Avenue, New York, New York 10110

Original edition © 2022 Mosquito Books, Barcelona
Text © 2022 Roger Vila
Translation © 2022 Paula Meiss
Illustrations © 2022 Rena Ortega
This edition © 2022 Thames & Hudson Ltd, London

British Library Cataloguing-in-Publication Data.
A catalogue record for this book is available from the British Library

Library of Congress Control Number 2021949739

ISBN 978-0-500-65301-2

Printed in Spain

FSC
www.fsc.org
MIX
Paper from
responsible sources
FSC® C104592

Be the first to know about our new releases,
exclusive content and author events by visiting
thamesandhudson.com
thamesandhudsonusa.com
thamesandhudson.com.au

The Secret Life of Butterflies

Roger Vila · Rena Ortega

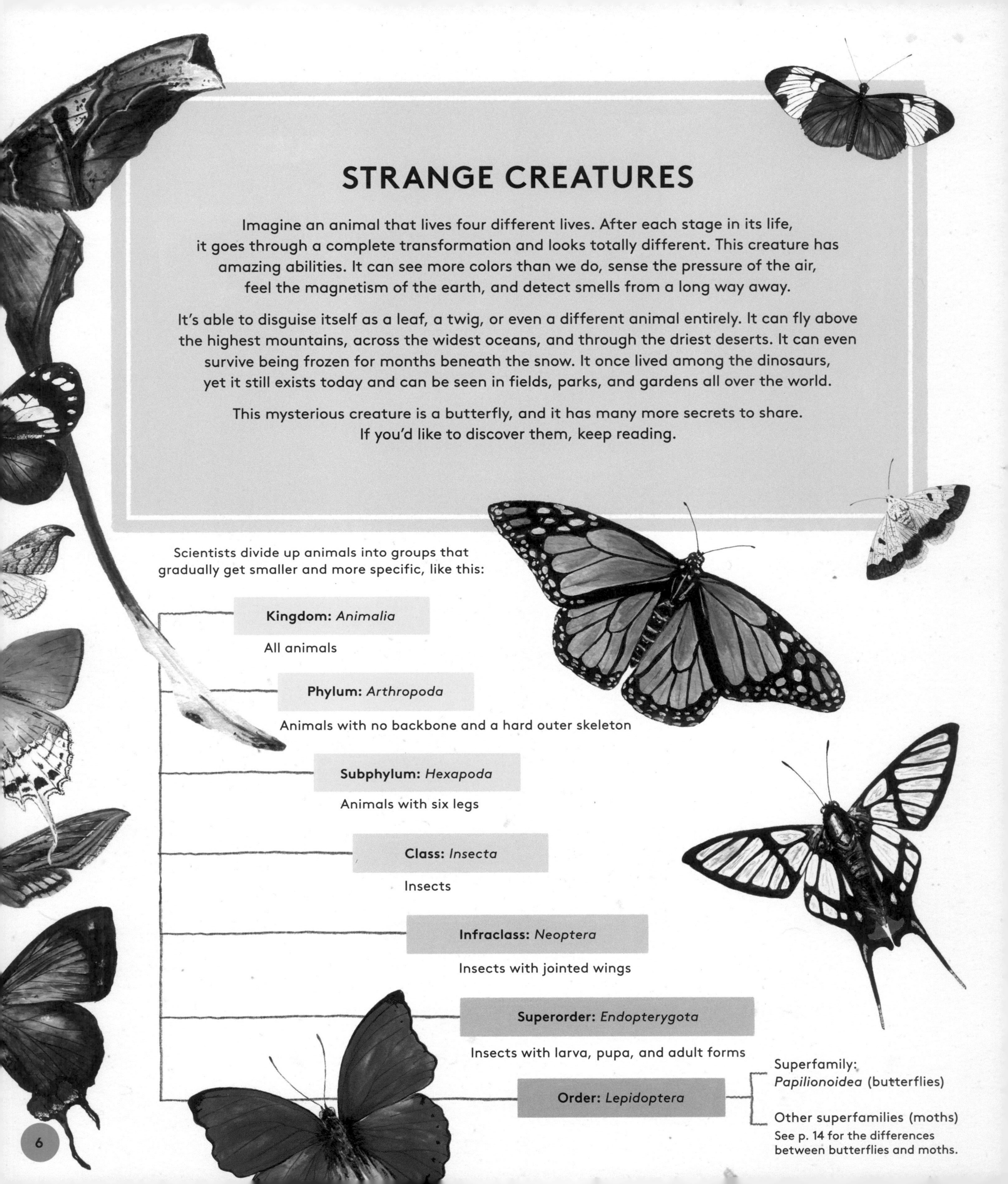

STRANGE CREATURES

Imagine an animal that lives four different lives. After each stage in its life,
it goes through a complete transformation and looks totally different. This creature has
amazing abilities. It can see more colors than we do, sense the pressure of the air,
feel the magnetism of the earth, and detect smells from a long way away.

It's able to disguise itself as a leaf, a twig, or even a different animal entirely. It can fly above
the highest mountains, across the widest oceans, and through the driest deserts. It can even
survive being frozen for months beneath the snow. It once lived among the dinosaurs,
yet it still exists today and can be seen in fields, parks, and gardens all over the world.

This mysterious creature is a butterfly, and it has many more secrets to share.
If you'd like to discover them, keep reading.

Scientists divide up animals into groups that
gradually get smaller and more specific, like this:

Kingdom: *Animalia*

All animals

Phylum: *Arthropoda*

Animals with no backbone and a hard outer skeleton

Subphylum: *Hexapoda*

Animals with six legs

Class: *Insecta*

Insects

Infraclass: *Neoptera*

Insects with jointed wings

Superorder: *Endopterygota*

Insects with larva, pupa, and adult forms

Order: *Lepidoptera*

Superfamily:
Papilionoidea (butterflies)

Other superfamilies (moths)
See p. 14 for the differences
between butterflies and moths.

SOME BUTTERFLY FAMILIES

PAPILIONIDAE

Better known as **swallowtails**, these large and colorful butterflies often have long "tails" on their hindwings.

HESPERIIDAE

Skippers are small butterflies with dull colors. They flap their wings very quickly when they fly.

PIERIDAE

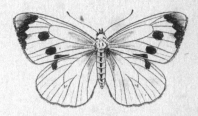

These medium-sized butterflies are quite common. They are often white or yellow.

NYMPHALIDAE

Also called **brush-footed butterflies**, these belong to the largest butterfly family. They tend to be large or medium in size and many are brown or orange with eyespots on their wings.

RIODINIDAE

These small colorful butterflies are also called **metalmarks**. Most of them live in the rainforests of South America.

LYCAENIDAE

This large family includes many small blue species. They are sometimes called **gossamer-winged butterflies**.

SOME MOTH FAMILIES

TORTRICIDAE

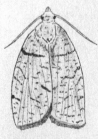

This family of small moths are also called **leafroller moths**.

EREBIDAE

Some of these medium-sized moths are very colorful. This warns predators that they are poisonous.

NOCTUIDAE

This large family are called **owlet moths**. Most are medium or small. They rest with their wings folded.

GEOMETRIDAE

Geometer moths rest with their wings wide open. Their caterpillars walk by stretching out their heads then moving their rear end forward, making a loop.

SPHINGIDAE

Commonly known as **hawk moths**, these moths have very long wings and can hover like hummingbirds.

SATURNIIDAE

This family includes the largest moths. They often have big eyespots on their wings.

BUTTERFLIES IN THE AGE OF DINOSAURS

Butterflies have lived on earth for over a hundred million years! Can you imagine butterflies fluttering among the dinosaurs? They weren't huge or ferocious, though. In fact, they were very similar to today's butterflies. Although they may look fragile, they managed to survive the major climate changes that wiped out the dinosaurs.

Voltinia dramba
In prehistoric times, butterflies sometimes died when they became trapped in the sticky resin of trees. Over millions of years, the resin fossilized and turned into amber. The fossils shown here are butterflies from the species *Voltinia dramba*, which lived 20 million years ago on a Caribbean island. Amber is transparent, so these rare butterflies can be studied in detail.

Prodryas persephone
Butterfly fossils are extremely rare. They are valuable not only because they're beautiful but also because scientists can learn a lot from them. This is one of the most famous fossils ever found. The butterfly is Prodryas persephone, which lived around 35 million years ago. When it died, it was compressed and turned to stone. It was the first butterfly fossil ever found in North America.

THROUGH A MAGNIFYING GLASS

What does a butterfly look like up close? Like all insects, butterflies have six legs, although the front two are sometimes very short. They also have four wings, and their body is divided into three sections: the head, the thorax, and the abdomen.

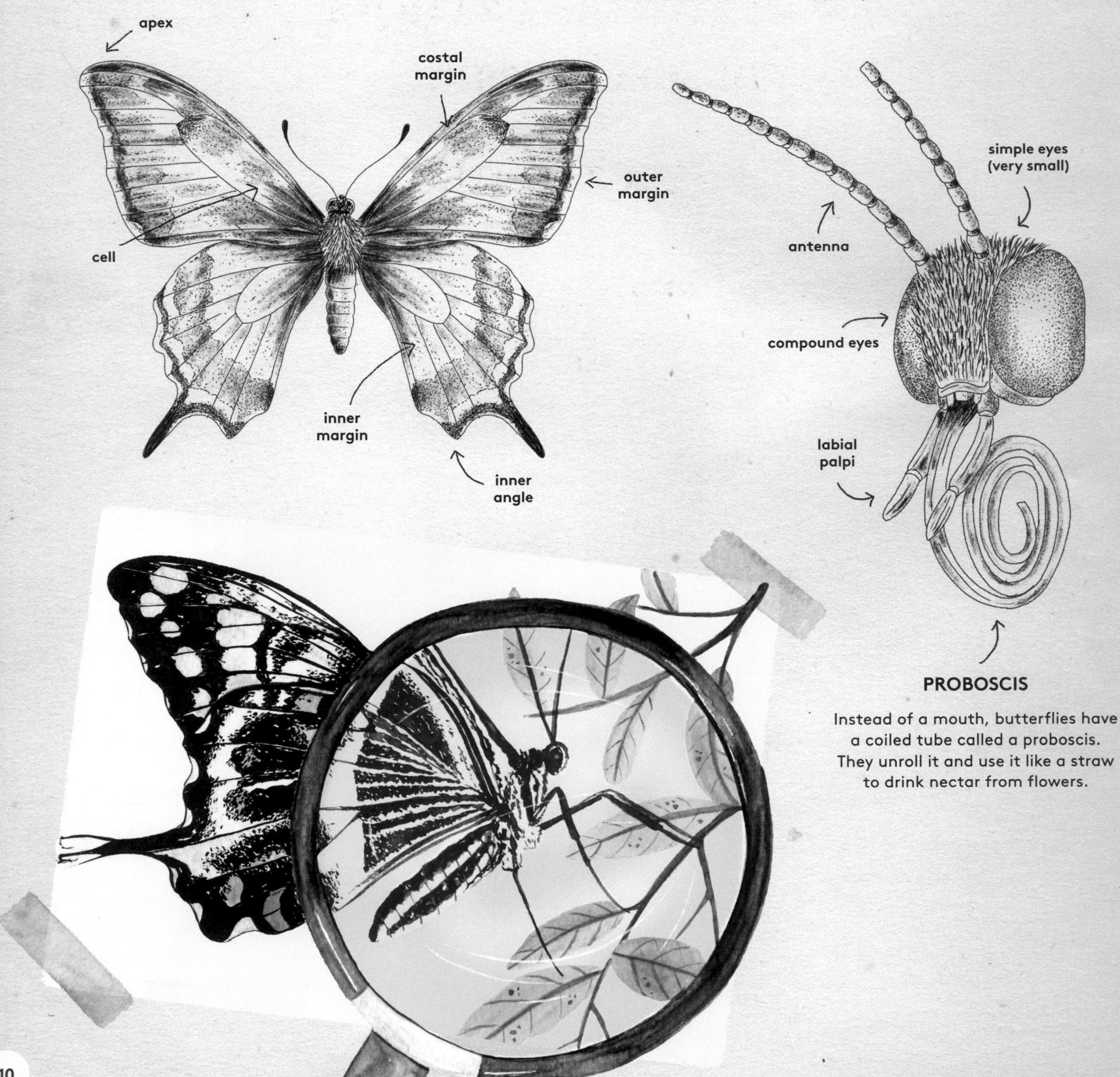

apex

costal margin

outer margin

cell

inner margin

inner angle

antenna

simple eyes (very small)

compound eyes

labial palpi

PROBOSCIS

Instead of a mouth, butterflies have a coiled tube called a proboscis. They unroll it and use it like a straw to drink nectar from flowers.

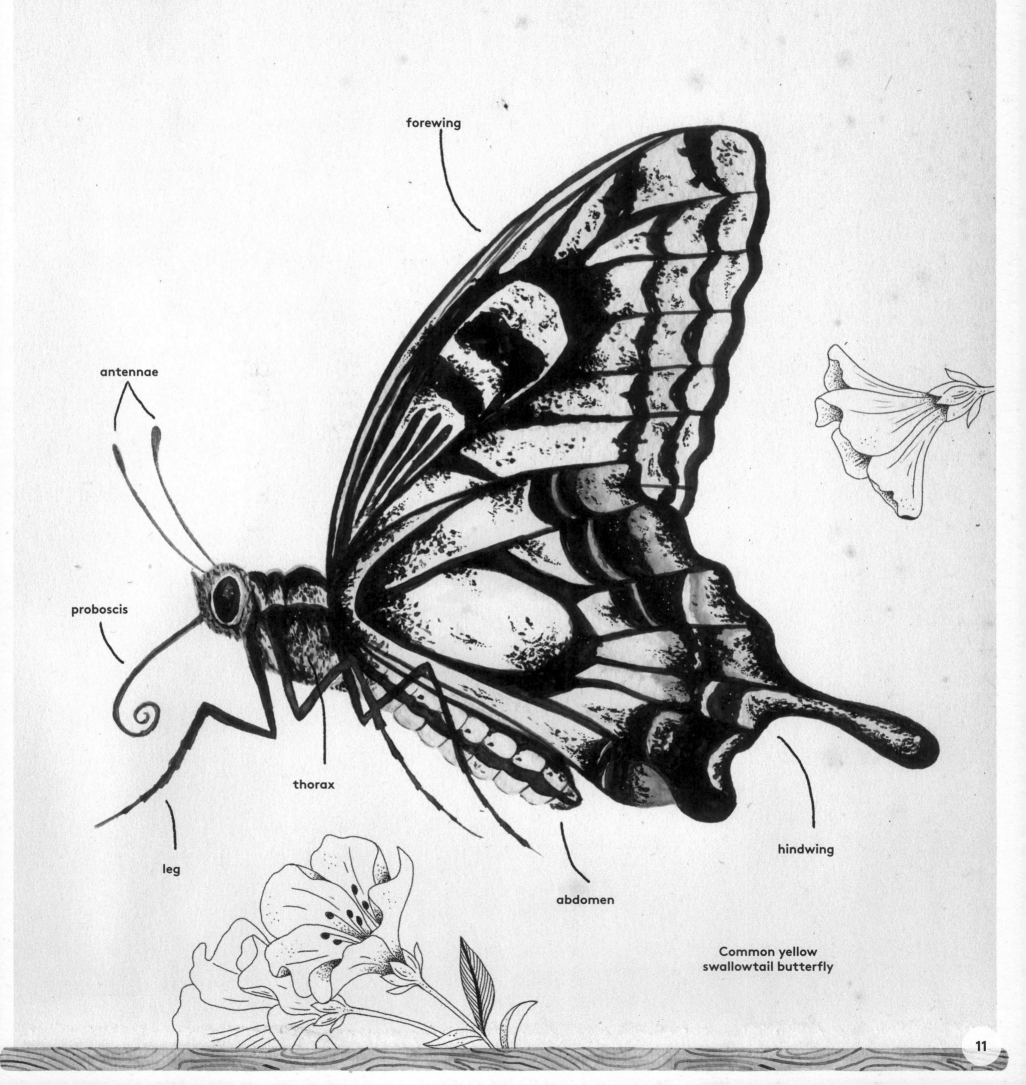

forewing

antennae

proboscis

leg

thorax

abdomen

hindwing

Common yellow
swallowtail butterfly

Common evening brown
This and many other butterflies from the *Satyrinae* family have brown wings. When they land on the ground with their wings open, they seem to disappear among the leaves and stones.

Geometer moth caterpillar
When this caterpillar is scared, it stretches out its body until it's stiff and straight, so it looks exactly like a twig. There are thousands of similar species. Their caterpillars may be brown, green, or gray to blend in with different plants.

Cracker butterfly
These butterflies like to rest on tree trunks, with their wings open and their heads facing the ground. Their shading acts as camouflage against the tree bark.

Comma butterfly
The brown wings of the comma are shaped like oak leaves. When these butterflies are resting, they stay very still and hide their antennae between their wings.

Urapia meticulodina
This moth's wings create an optical illusion. They look like dried leaves with curling edges, but it's just a clever pattern. In fact, their wings are completely flat.

MASTERS OF CAMOUFLAGE

Predators will eat any butterflies and caterpillars they can find, so hiding in plain sight is a good way to survive. After millions of years of evolution, some species have become true masters of camouflage!

How do they do it? Color is important, but the key to looking exactly like a twig or a leaf is posing in the right way.

Oakleaf butterfly
When their wings are folded, these butterflies look exactly like leaves. They usually rest on dead leaves or tree branches, where they are hard to spot. There are several species and each one imitates a different kind of leaf.

Common baron caterpillar
When they sit on a leaf, their long transparent bodies blend into the leaf's central rib.

Emerald moth
These geometer moths rest with their wings wide open and blend in with their surroundings. The green ones rest on leaves, the brown ones rest on tree trunks, and the white and gray ones rest on rocks and lichen.

Glasswing butterfly
Their wings are transparent because their wing scales have shrunk to the size of tiny hairs. They live in dark tropical forests, where it is very hard to see them.

BUTTERFLIES AND MOTHS: WHAT'S THE DIFFERENCE?

Butterflies and moths are part of a group of insects called *Lepidoptera*. Butterflies fly in the daytime, are usually brightly colored, and have smooth antennae with thicker tips.

Moths usually fly at night and have fewer colors, but this is not true of all moth species. Some are active during the day and some are even as colorful as butterflies. Their antennae may be thin and threadlike or broad and featherlike.

Ulysses butterfly

Polyphemus
moth

Scientists who study
butterflies and moths are
called **lepidopterists**.

LET'S FLY!

Everyone knows that butterflies can fly, but
did you know that they can fly in three different ways?

Flapping
Most species fly by
flapping their wings about
five times a second.

**Cabbage white
butterfly**

**White-lined
sphinx moth**

Hovering
Some species of moths beat their wings up to
45 times every second. Try it with your arms:
that is very fast! Hummingbird moths have
long, narrow wings and look like a hummingbird.
They can pirouette, hover, and fly faster than others.
However, flying in this way needs a lot of energy, so the
moths must feed from lots of flowers afterward.

NOT ALL MOTHS FLY!

Some female moths have no wings or wings that are too small to fly. They wait quietly for a male moth to find them. After they mate, the females lay their eggs on the same plant where they lived as caterpillars.

Gliding
Species with large wings can glide on the wind. They hardly need to move their wings, so they don't waste energy.

Common green birdwing

MASTERS OF DISGUISE

Not all butterflies hide to avoid being eaten. Some species disguise themselves as dangerous animals. If they look like a poisonous snake, a wasp, or an owl with huge eyes, no predator will dare to come near!

Owl butterfly
It is easy to tell how this butterfly got its name. The round spots on its wings look like owl eyes and scare off small predators. It is a very large butterfly, measuring about 5½ in across.

The trick of imitating another species is called **mimicry**. One butterfly will copy the colors and patterns of another insect or animal that is poisonous or tastes bad, so birds will not eat it.

Io moth
Some butterflies and moths have round dots on their wings, called eyespots. They look like the eyes of an owl, and scare away predators such as mice, birds, and lizards.

Blue jay
This bird loves to eat butterflies and caterpillars, but most of the butterflies it finds are protected by their disguises. To study how butterflies can trick predators, scientists carry out experiments using tame birds.

Hemeroplanes triptolemus
The caterpillar of this large hawk moth scares away predators by pretending to be a poisonous snake. It does this by making its tail end swell up so that it looks exactly like the head of a snake. It even has black patches where the snake's eyes should be.

Hornet moth
Is it a hornet or a wasp? No, it's a hornet moth! The yellow and black stripes on its body and the long transparent wings make it an almost perfect copy of a stinging wasp. This means that predators stay away.

Giant swallowtail caterpillar
Some young caterpillars look exactly like bird droppings. When they're lying on a leaf, no predator wants to touch them, let alone eat them!

Hairstreak butterfly
Many butterflies have bright and glossy colors and shapes on the backs of their wings. These attract the attention of predators, which may attack the butterfly's wings. However, even if a piece of its wing is broken off, the butterfly can still escape. Can you see a fake insect head, with eyes and antennae, growing on the back of this butterfly's wing?

BUTTERFLY SUPERPOWERS

Did you know butterflies have superpowers? For example, their eyes can capture ultraviolet light, so they can see more colors than we do. They see a wider rainbow, with more colors after violet that human eyes can't detect.

The antennae of butterflies and moths come in three main shapes. Butterflies have straight antennae with a thicker tip at the end. Most moths have antennae that are thin and threadlike. However, the males of some moths have feathery antennae, which they use to detect the scent of female moths at night.

FEMALE MOTH
threadlike antennae

MALE MOTH
feathery antennae

BUTTERFLY
club-shaped antennae

This is how a human sees a flower.

This is how a butterfly sees the same flower.

Flowers that humans see as plain white or yellow have spots and patterns that only butterflies can see. Each species of butterfly only visits the types of flowers it likes best.

Butterflies can feel the pressure of the air so they know if the weather will be clear or stormy. Some of them can also feel the earth's magnetic field. This means that they can tell which direction is north, and can find their way when migrating.

A butterfly's eyes can see shades that humans cannot see.

Butterflies have an amazing sense of smell. They have "noses" all over their bodies: on their antennae, on their legs, and on the tip of their abdomen. They use these "noses" to smell plants and choose the best places to lay their eggs. They also use smell to find a mate of their own species to breed with.

Spotted fritillary

In America, painted ladies fly all the way from Canada to Mexico to escape from the cold winter weather.

AN EPIC JOURNEY

Some butterflies migrate in the same way that some birds and other animals do. When it is too hot or too cold, or when there is no food, they fly away to find a better place to live. Every year, butterflies of the same species make the same journey along the same route.

Painted lady butterflies can be found almost everywhere in the world and make the most incredible migration journeys. Every summer, millions of them are born in northern Europe and then fly across the Sahara Desert to breed on the African savannah. When the plants dry up there, the children and grandchildren of the original painted ladies fly back to Europe.

In Asia, painted ladies migrate from Siberia to India and southern China, crossing the Himalayas and flying at thousands of feet above sea level.

HOW DO MIGRATING BUTTERFLIES FIND THEIR WAY?

This is a mystery that scientists are still trying to solve. However, one very surprising fact has already been discovered. Butterflies have a sort of internal compass, so they can always sense which direction is north.

BUTTERFLY RECORDS

The world's largest butterfly is the Queen Alexandra's birdwing from Papua New Guinea. The females, which are larger than the males, have a wingspan of 11 inches.

The largest moth is the white witch from South America. It can grow up to 12 inches across, although other species can weigh more.

White witch moth
South America
12 in

Queen Alexandra's
birdwing
Papua New Guinea
11 in

Micropsyche ariana
Afghanistan
¼ in

The smallest butterfly species is *Micropsyche ariana*.
It is very rare, comes from Afghanistan, and measures about ¾ inch.

Midget moths are the smallest family of moths. The smallest ones are
less than ¼ inch across! You need a magnifying glass to see them.

Midget moth

¼ in   ¾ in

WHICH BUTTERFLY FLIES THE FASTEST?

The fastest butterflies are the skippers, and the fastest moths are the hawk moths. Both can fly at speeds of 37 miles per hour, almost as fast as a horse.

62 mph

37 mph

Not even the fastest human runner in the world could catch them!

28 mph

WHICH BUTTERFLY FLIES THE FURTHEST?

Every year, millions of painted lady butterflies travel from tropical Africa to the Arctic Circle and back, on a round trip that's 7,500 miles long. They breed and die along the way and it takes six to ten generations of butterflies to complete the whole journey. However, a single butterfly can also fly a long way in its short life: with the help of the wind, it can travel up to 2,500 miles.

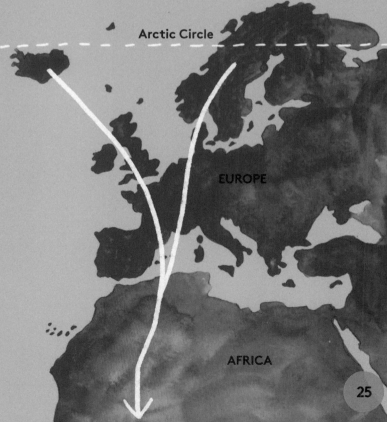

Arctic Circle

EUROPE

AFRICA

11 in   12 in

Adult butterflies normally drink nectar from flowers, which they sip with their proboscis. But they can also drink the juice from ripe fruit, sap from tree trunks, or honey from beehives.

WHAT DO BUTTERFLIES EAT?

Caterpillars normally eat leaves, but they are very fussy. Each species will only eat a few specific plants. Some caterpillars have more unusual tastes and will eat flowers, fruit, or wood. A few are carnivores and eat other insects. There are even some cannibal caterpillars that eat their own brothers and sisters!

FASCINATING FACT

Some moths don't have mouths and never eat. They survive on the food they ate while they were caterpillars.

Male butterflies gather in large numbers on damp soil to drink mineral salts from the earth. They can get the same salts from animal pee or droppings and even from the bodies of dead animals. If a butterfly lands on your arm, it might want to drink your sweat. Butterflies think it's tasty!

A BUTTERFLY LOVE STORY

Adult butterflies and moths live just for a few weeks. Their most important job is to mate and lay eggs. In that short time, they can have many children—sometimes hundreds and hundreds!

The first step is to find a partner of the same species. With so many different species, this is not an easy task. Male butterflies find a potential mate by color. However, it is the female who makes the final choice. Usually she uses her antennae to smell the male and work out if he is the right partner for her. Some species perform a sort of mating dance, either in the air or on the ground.

Monarch butterflies

Butterflies mate by joining the ends of their abdomens together, with each partner facing in a different direction. They can stay like this for hours. They usually stand still, but many species can take off and fly while mating, especially if something scares them suddenly.

DID YOU KNOW?

Pheromones are the natural scents that butterflies and other animals use to attract a mate.

Spanish moon moth

How do moths find mates at night? Male moths have featherlike antennae that can detect the scent of female moths from a long way away. Each species has a different smell. This means that the night air is full of scents that humans can't detect.

Cecropia moths mating

BUTTERFLY EGGS

All butterflies and moths lay eggs, although in some cases caterpillars may hatch from eggs inside the female.

If you look at the eggs through a magnifying glass, you will see that the eggs of each species come in different shapes and colors. Some of them look like little jewels. They protect the caterpillar growing inside from heat and rain, while still allowing it to breathe.

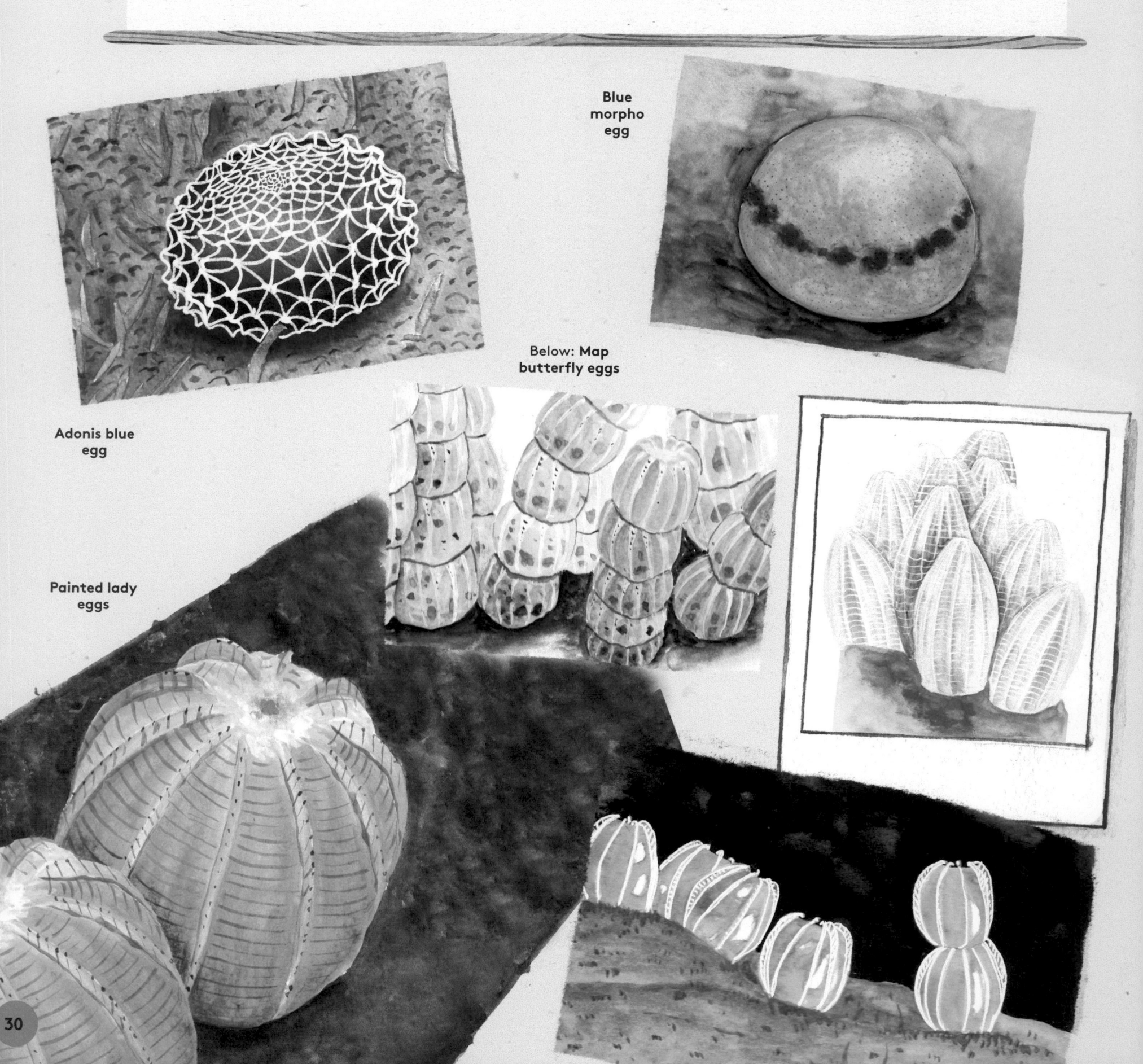

Blue morpho egg

Adonis blue egg

Below: Map butterfly eggs

Painted lady eggs

Io moth eggs

FOUR LIVES IN ONE

Did you know that all butterflies go through four completely different stages of life? They begin as an egg, then become a caterpillar, then a pupa, and eventually an adult butterfly. This series of changes can take between one month and several years.

Luna moth eggs

Lesser owl butterfly eggs

The egg's color may change over time. Just before the caterpillar hatches, the egg becomes transparent and the tiny caterpillar can be seen inside.

Monarch caterpillar hatching

CATERPILLARS

Caterpillars have only one job—to grow. And they do it very quickly! They are extremely hungry and usually eat plants. They have long bodies and large heads with strong jaws for chewing. Their six short legs are close to their head and the rest of their body has false legs covered in tiny hooks, which they use for grasping and walking.

Because lots of creatures want to eat caterpillars, many of them have evolved into amazing shapes and startling shades in order to scare away predators. Here is a selection of some of the most unusual caterpillars in the world!

Hickory horned moth caterpillar

Cecropia moth caterpillar

Lobster moth caterpillar

Wattle cup caterpillar

Limacodid slug caterpillar

Euphobetron moth
caterpillar

Spicebush
swallowtail
caterpillar

Guatemalan
cracker caterpillar

Spurge hawk moth
caterpillar

Pacific fruit-
piercing moth
caterpillar

Puss moth
caterpillar

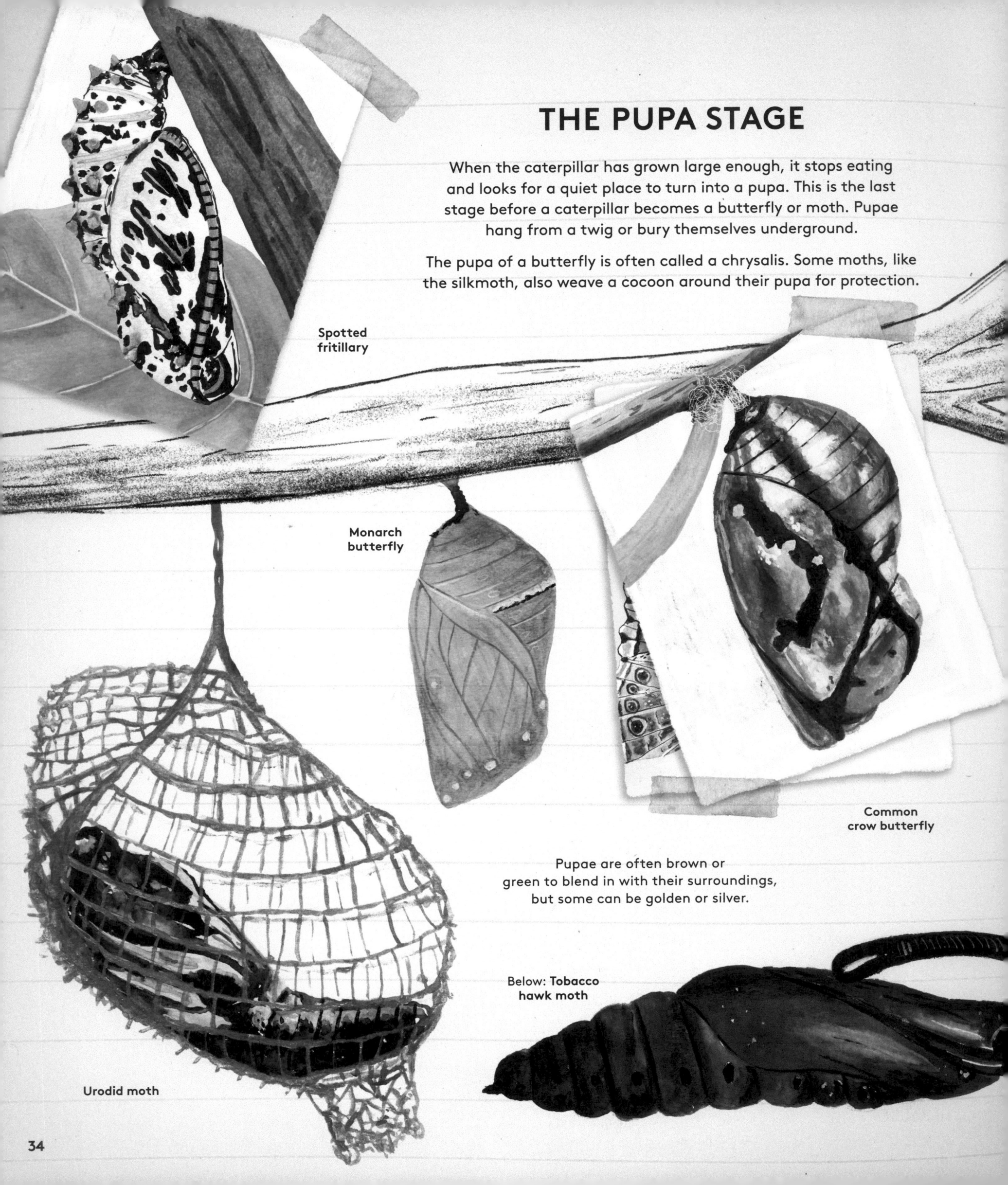

THE PUPA STAGE

When the caterpillar has grown large enough, it stops eating and looks for a quiet place to turn into a pupa. This is the last stage before a caterpillar becomes a butterfly or moth. Pupae hang from a twig or bury themselves underground.

The pupa of a butterfly is often called a chrysalis. Some moths, like the silkmoth, also weave a cocoon around their pupa for protection.

Spotted fritillary

Monarch butterfly

Common crow butterfly

Pupae are often brown or green to blend in with their surroundings, but some can be golden or silver.

Below: Tobacco hawk moth

Urodid moth

34

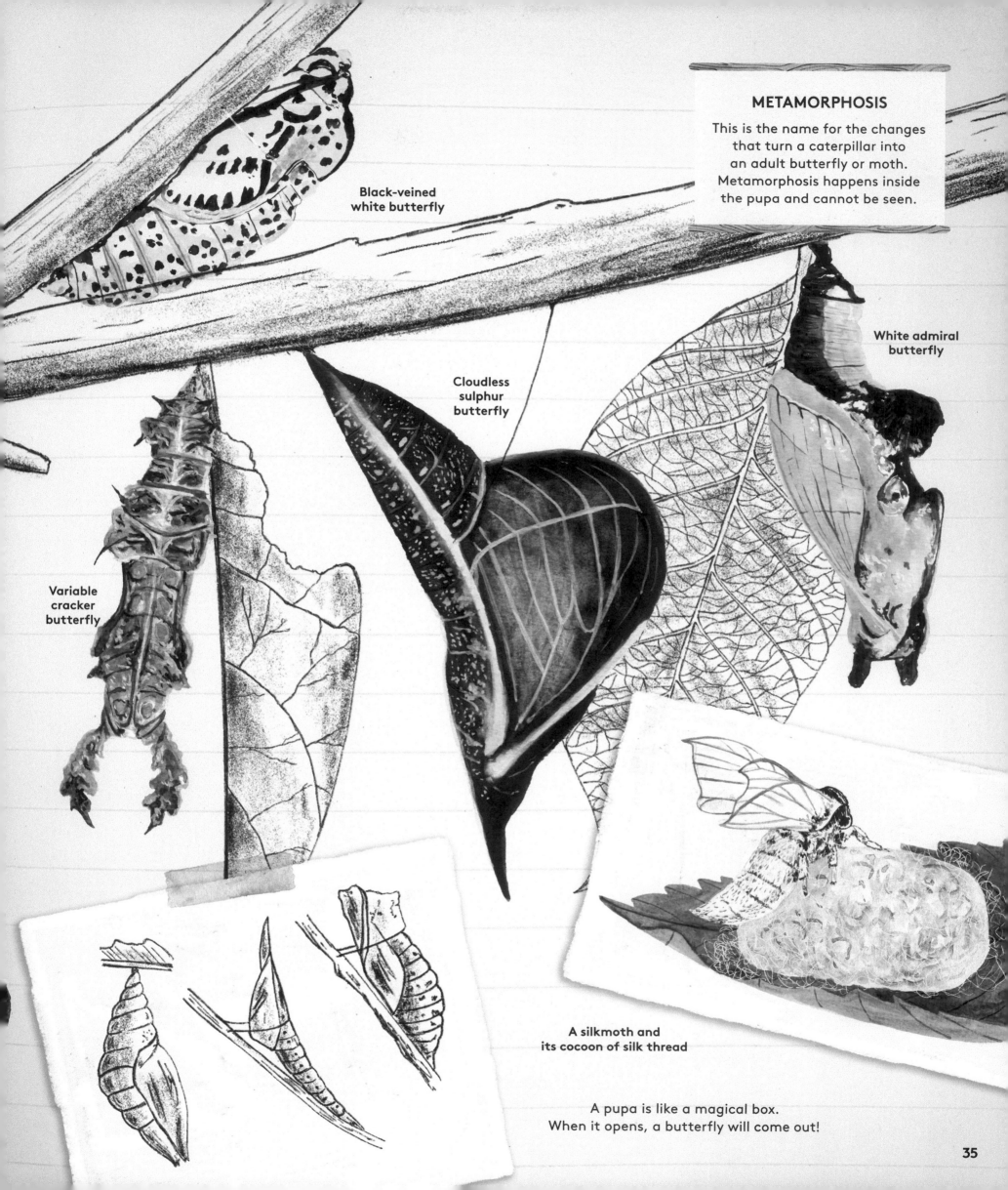

Black-veined
white butterfly

METAMORPHOSIS
This is the name for the changes
that turn a caterpillar into
an adult butterfly or moth.
Metamorphosis happens inside
the pupa and cannot be seen.

White admiral
butterfly

Cloudless
sulphur
butterfly

Variable
cracker
butterfly

A silkmoth and
its cocoon of silk thread

A pupa is like a magical box.
When it opens, a butterfly will come out!

WHERE DO BUTTERFLIES GO WHEN IT'S COLD?

Butterflies only fly when it is sunny and warm. If it rains, they prefer not to move around, but nothing happens to them because their wings are waterproof. Many butterflies, like other insects, can go into a deep sleep when they feel the cold of winter coming. This protects them from snow and frost.

Pine processionary caterpillars in a communal nest

Camberwell beauty

Peacock butterfly

Some species spend the winter as adult butterflies, sheltering in caves, or among plants. On sunny days, these butterflies wake up, fly to warm themselves up and look for a flower to feed on.

Most butterflies and moths spend the winter as eggs, caterpillars or pupae. Buried under the snowy ground, they may look dead, but when the spring comes, they will wake up and become active again. Some caterpillars weave communal silk nests in trees, for extra protection.

DIAPAUSE

The diapause is when a butterfly seems to be sleeping or hibernating. It can survive very low temperatures in winter and very high temperatures in summer.

BEAUTIFUL DIVERSITY

There are around 200,000 species of butterflies and moths in the world. They come in all sorts of shapes and sizes, and scientists discover new species every year. Butterflies can be found on every continent except Antarctica, because it is too cold there and there are no flowers to feed from.

1. Southern dogface butterfly (North America)   2. Madagascan sunset moth (Madagascar)   3. Adonis blue butterfly (Europe)
4. Malaysian moon moth (Asia)   5. Heady maiden moth (Africa)   6. Blood-red glider butterfly (Africa)

7. Blushing phantom butterfly (South America)   8. Death's-head hawk moth (Europe and Africa)   9. Long-tailed metalmark (South America)
10. Obi Island birdwing butterfly (Indonesia)   11. Postman butterfly (Central & North America)   12. Common mapwing butterfly (Asia)

THE WORLD NEEDS BUTTERFLIES

Butterflies are not only beautiful and fascinating, but very important.
Without them, the delicate balance of nature would be disrupted.
Here are some of the jobs they do in nature.

They are a source of food for many other
animals. Birds, reptiles, small mammals,
and other insects all feed on them. For
example, bats mostly eat moths. Without
butterflies and moths, many of these
animals could not survive.

Caterpillars eat lots and lots of plants and help to control their growth. If there were no caterpillars, some plants would grow too fast and threaten other species.

When butterflies fly from flower to flower, they carry pollen with them, which the plants use to reproduce. Without butterflies, many plants would have no way to make new seeds.

41

SAVE THE BUTTERFLIES

Butterflies are at risk all over the world.
There are fewer of them every year and some species are
already extinct. But there are things we can do to save them.
Here are some dangers that they face and some ways you can help.

PESTICIDES

Farms often spray chemicals on their crops to stop insects from eating
them. However, these chemicals also kill butterflies. Because of this,
it's best to eat organic products, which are grown without pesticides.

CLIMATE CHANGE

Global warming is killing butterflies in mountain areas, which have
adapted to live in the cold. Global warming also creates droughts, which
kill the flowers that butterflies feed from. Climate change is caused by
using too much gas and oil, so it's important not to waste energy:

1) Turn off lights and other electrical items that you don't need.

2) Use public transportation, bike, or walk whenever you can.

3) Buy from stores close to where you live. Try to avoid products
that have to be transported from a long way away.

HABITAT LOSS

Places where butterflies like to live, especially flower meadows, are often
destroyed to build houses and roads. If you plant flowers in your garden or
grow them on your balcony or windowsill, butterflies will feed from them.
If you see caterpillars eating the leaves of your plants, it's a great chance
to take a closer look—but don't touch them!

GLOSSARY

Antennae: The two feelers on a butterfly's head.

Abdomen: The end section of a butterfly's body.

Carnivore: An animal that eats other animals.

Chrysalis: Another word for the pupa of a butterfly.

Cocoon: A protective layer of silk woven around the pupa of a moth.

Diapause: A state that is similar to hibernation. A butterfly can begin a diapause when the temperature changes or when there is not enough water or food. It stops moving and seems to be asleep.

Eyespot: A marking that looks like an eye. These can sometimes be found on the wings of butterflies and birds, or on the skin of fish and reptiles. They are used as a way to scare predators, who think there's a bigger animal watching them.

Forewings: The two front wings of a butterfly.

Fossil: The remains of an ancient plant or animal, preserved inside rock.

Habitat: The place where an animal lives.

Herbivore: An animal that eats plants.

Hindwings: The two back wings of a butterfly.

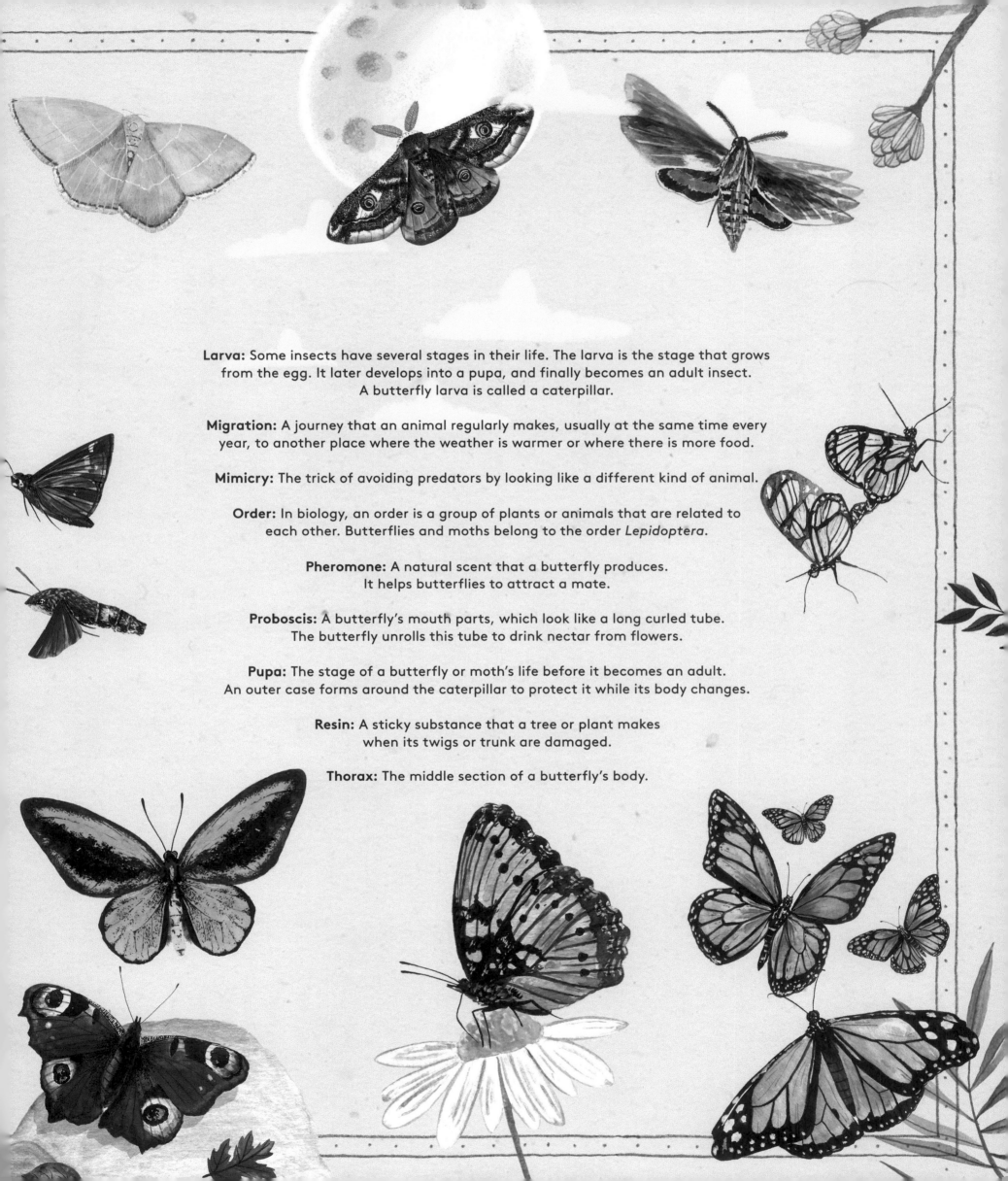

Larva: Some insects have several stages in their life. The larva is the stage that grows from the egg. It later develops into a pupa, and finally becomes an adult insect. A butterfly larva is called a caterpillar.

Migration: A journey that an animal regularly makes, usually at the same time every year, to another place where the weather is warmer or where there is more food.

Mimicry: The trick of avoiding predators by looking like a different kind of animal.

Order: In biology, an order is a group of plants or animals that are related to each other. Butterflies and moths belong to the order *Lepidoptera*.

Pheromone: A natural scent that a butterfly produces. It helps butterflies to attract a mate.

Proboscis: A butterfly's mouth parts, which look like a long curled tube. The butterfly unrolls this tube to drink nectar from flowers.

Pupa: The stage of a butterfly or moth's life before it becomes an adult. An outer case forms around the caterpillar to protect it while its body changes.

Resin: A sticky substance that a tree or plant makes when its twigs or trunk are damaged.

Thorax: The middle section of a butterfly's body.